LLAMA CRAFTS

Racehorse Publishing books may be purchased in bulk at special discounts for sales promotion, corporate gifts, fund-raising, or educational purposes. Special editions can also be created to specifications. For details, contact the Special Sales Department, Skyhorse Publishing, 307 West 36th Street, 11th Floor, New York, NY 10018 or info@skyhorsepublishing.com.

Racehorse Publishing™ is a pending trademark of Skyhorse Publishing, Inc.®, a Delaware corporation.

Visit our website at www.skyhorsepublishing.com.

10 9 8 7 6 5 4 3 2 1

Library of Congress Cataloging-in-Publication Data is available on file.

Cover and interior design by Antonia Orrego Requena
Cover photography by Pilar Castro Evensen

Print ISBN: 978-1-63158-449-7
E-Book ISBN: 978-1-63158-450-3

Printed in China

LLAMA CRAFTS

By Ellen Deakin

of Happythought

Racehorse Publishing

CONTENTS

INTRODUCTION

Welcome to *Llama Crafts*! I'm so happy that you are here and so excited to share these llama craft projects with you.

I'm guessing you love llamas as much as I do. If so, you're in luck! There are all sorts of llamas in this book—cute llamas, elegant llamas, funny llamas, and cuddly llamas—llamas that are so full of personality!

I've had some help along the way from many talented friends. We've had a lot of fun putting together these projects for you, so I hope you enjoy using this book as much as we enjoyed creating it!

Have a llama-tastic day,

Ellen

The projects in this book are rated from easy to advanced and there is also an indication of how long each project will take. You can tell which project has a template too.

Easy   Medium   Hard

Time needed   Includes templates

SO WHAT IS A LLAMA?

A llama is like a camel without a hump, but it also has a woolly coat.
A llama is domesticated—it isn't wild and always belongs to someone.

Where do llamas live? Llamas come from the high mountains of the Andes in South American countries. Most llamas live in or near the Andes. Other countries now breed llamas for their wool, to use as pack animals on ranches, and even as guardians for herds of sheep. Another reason for bringing llamas to other countries is llama therapy. Grown-ups and children can get a lot of help from contact and friendship with a llama!

Why do people keep llamas? In the past and in the mountains they were used as pack animals. They are big and strong with flat backs—perfect for loading up with a pack of goods for transport through mountain landscapes! Today, llamas are kept and bred for their wool. Their wool is warmer than sheep wool and less itchy. It is naturally "hypoallergenic" so less likely to cause allergies.

Why do we love llamas? Could it be their funny faces? They look quite human in some ways, but their big eyes and banana ears make them look surprised all the time. Also, they are woolly in an untidy, comical way. Even their movements are comical, although they are fast and powerful as well. They are super intelligent and can learn routines. They live in close families like us.

MEET THE LLAMA'S COUSINS!

ALPACA

GUANACO

VICUÑA

Llamas are domesticated and their closest cousin is the alpaca. Then there are their wild, undomesticated cousins. Guanacos are a bigger, wild forebear of the llama and vicuñas are more closely related to the alpaca. Neither of these are exported to other countries, so they only live in South America.

Do you know the difference between a llama and an alpaca? Alpacas are smaller—about half the size of a llama. They have straight, spear-shaped ears rather than the llama's banana ears, and a slightly humped back which stops them from being used as pack animals. Llamas have a longer face. An alpaca's wool is even finer than that of a llama.

Have you heard of the Guanaco and the Vicuña? They are mainly wild mountain animals. They can run up very steep slopes, and are very beautiful to watch in movement. Guanacos are big—standing approximately between 5 and 6 feet. Their colors are shades of reddish brown, whereas vicuñas vary from cinnamon brown to white.

LLAMA YARN AND FABRIC CRAFTS

Fabric in various colors

Ribbon

Colorful felt

Yarn for pom-poms

Embroidery thread for colorful tassels

Embroidery needles

Twine

A sharp pair of scissors

Colorful fabric paint

Cushion stuffing

LLAMA PAPER CRAFTS

Tissue paper
Gluc stick
White liquid glue
Cardboard
Colored card stock
Contact film

Colored pens and pencils
Acrylic paint
Paint brushes
Clear tape and masking tape
Foam sheets
Glitter

HAPPY LLAMA STAMPERS

🦙🦙🦙🦙🦙 ◗ 30 min.

Make these easy stamps using foam sheets from your local craft store.
Create your own wrapping paper, wall art, garlands,
greeting cards, and more!

The effect is wonderful, a little rustic, and very versatile.
Look after your stamps and you can use them over
and over again.

YOU WILL NEED:

Craft foam sheets
A ballpoint pen
Scrap cardboard
Scissors
White glue
Paint and paintbrushes

HOW TO MAKE YOUR STAMPS:

1.

Choose the image you want to make. You can use our templates in this book or create your own and transfer the design onto the foam sheet.

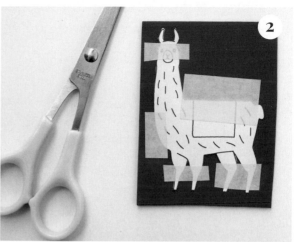

2.

You can either draw straight onto the foam or trace around one of the templates using a ballpoint pen. Press firmly so it marks directly on the foam or leaves an indent that you can retrace. Carefully cut out around the shape. Be sure that you are using nice sharp scissors.

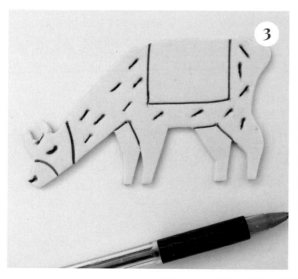

3.

Now, flip the foam shape over. To create detail on your stamp, use a ballpoint pen to sketch indentations. Remember that the lines you draw will be reversed when you print.

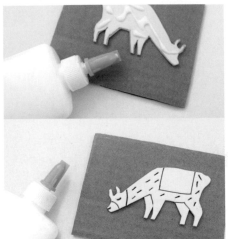

4.

Next, glue your foam shape onto a scrap piece of cardboard to give it more weight. Add a handle (as shown above) using further scraps of cardboard. Prepare several stamps. We made a cactus, a sun, and some packages for the llama to carry!

Prepare your paint. Using a brush, cover the stamp with a thin layer of the color. When you're ready to use them, brush a light coat of acrylic or fabric paint across the foam and then firmly press down on the object you're stamping.

It's a good idea to practice on a blank piece of paper first so you can get a feel for how much paint to use.

TIP!

Use the eraser on the top of a pencil to make circles for pom-poms.

—

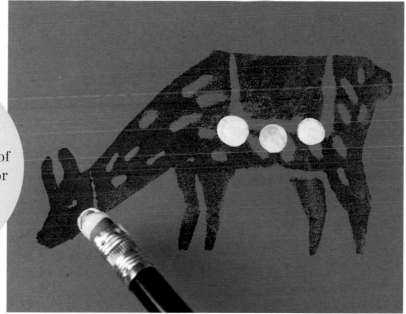

PROJECT 2:

LLAMA WEAVING

 ●● 1–2 hours

These rustic little llamas are fun and easy to make!
Make your own weaving loom using sticks from your garden or park,
or lollipop sticks from the craft shop.

Next, pick some colorful wool and yarn and get weaving!
You can vary the size and make a whole family of woven llamas.
Hang them on the wall as sweet decorations.

YOU WILL NEED:

Wooden sticks
Yarn
An embroidery needle
Scissors
Glue
Pruning shears

HOW TO MAKE
YOUR LLAMA WEAVING:

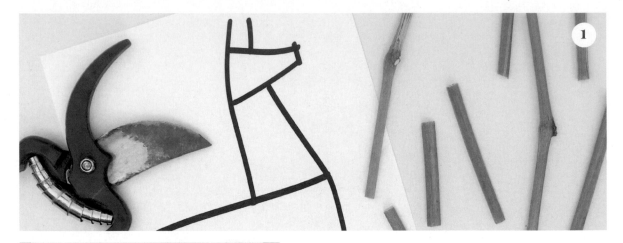

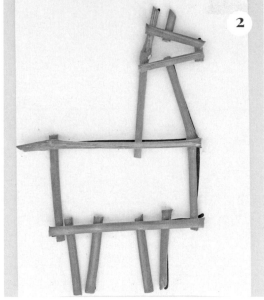

1.

Sketch out your llama and cut the
sticks to the length needed.
You may need to use pruning shears.

2.

Lay the sticks in place
over your sketch.

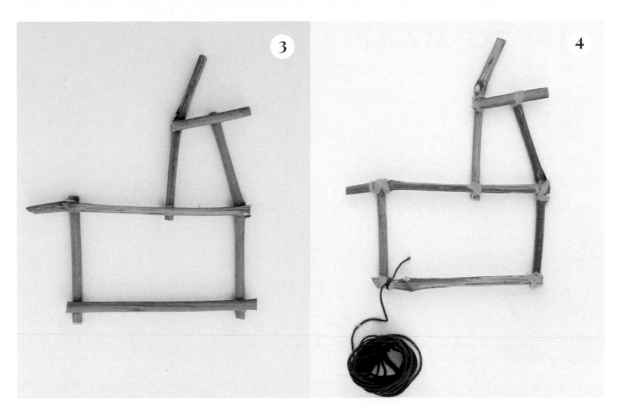

3. To make the frame for your weaving, glue together the main sticks as shown.

4. Bind the corners together with a little yarn.

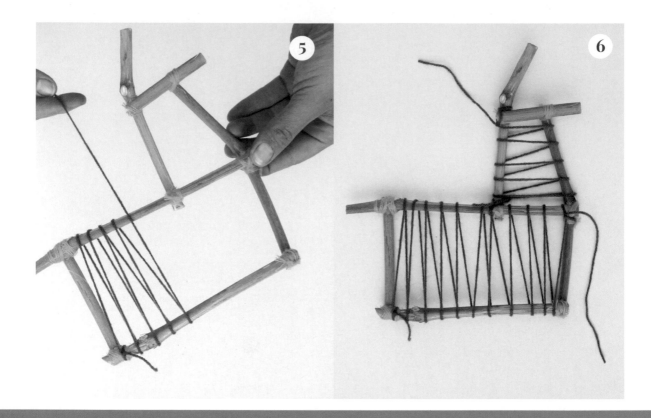

5. Wrap a length of yarn around the bottom rectangle as shown, securing with a knot.

6. Repeat this process on the neck of the llama frame.

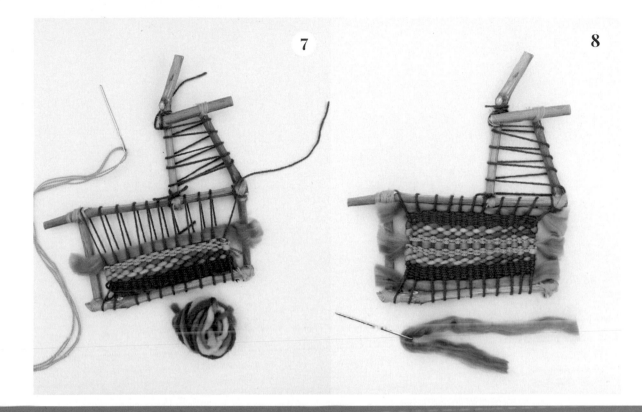

7. Take your embroidery needle with a length of thread. Attach the thread with a knot and begin to weave in and out of the strands.

8. Repeat this process with different colors and widths of yarn.

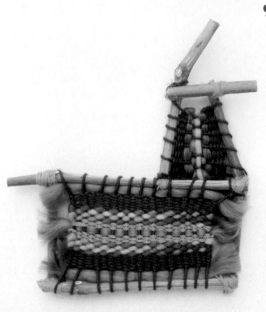

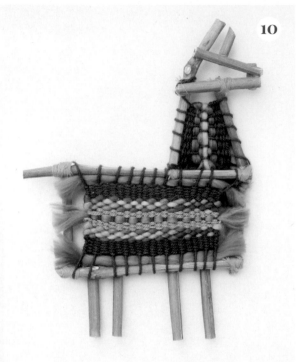

9.

Next, weave in between the strands of the neck.

10.

Glue the remaining sticks in place.

PAPER SUN-CATCHERS

  30 min.

Make these glorious and colorful sun-catchers to decorate a window or door in your home.

They are fun and easy to make and will look jewel-like with the sun shining through, like mini stained-glass windows. This is a fun craft for younger children. They will need a little help to cut out the llama base, then let them loose to have fun preparing and sticking on the colorful strips of tissue paper.

YOU WILL NEED:

Black or colored card stock
Colorful tissue paper
Transparent film
Ballpoint pen
White pencil (or similar)
Sticky tape

HOW TO MAKE A SUN-CATCHER:

1.

To make the base for your sun-catcher you can use the templates in this book or create your own llama design. The first step is to draw your design on a sheet of black card stock using a white pencil. Or you can transfer the design onto card stock using a ballpoint pen. Tape the design onto the card stock and, pressing hard, trace around the llama outline. This will leave an indentation for you to cut around. Once you have cut out your first template, you can then draw around it to create more.

2.

Carefully cut around the templates and interior shapes using scissors or a craft knife. Lay your card stock template face down onto a sheet of clear contact paper or, if you don't have any contact paper, you can use strips from a wide roll of transparent sticky tape.

3.

Prepare your colorful tissue paper by cutting or tearing it into pieces.

Now to have fun with your colors! Lay the colored paper all over, as shown. Don't worry if it overlaps; this adds to the effect!

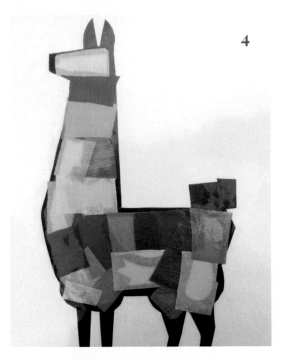

4

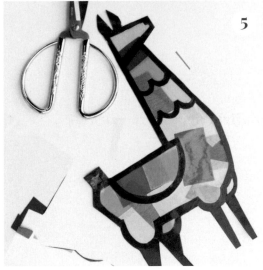

5

4.

Next, lay a second sheet of contact paper, sticky side down, on top of your colorful llama.

5.

Carefully cut around the llama, trimming off overlapping tissue paper.

6. Hooray! Your llama sun catchers are now ready to hang in the window!

7. You can attach them to the window using small strips of the contact paper, sticky tape, or a lightweight spray adhesive.

LLAMA PLUSH

2 hours.

Make your own adorable llama plush!
These cuddly plushies are easy to make and full of character.
Add accessories to your llama and dress it up your own way with
tassels, pom-poms, and fabric scraps.

These cuddly plushies will look great on your bed or sofa.
We also made a cute mountain cushion covered in pom-poms!

YOU WILL NEED:

Fun fur fabric
Cushion filling
Needle and thread
Scissors
Fabric scraps
Tassels and pom-poms
Fabric glue

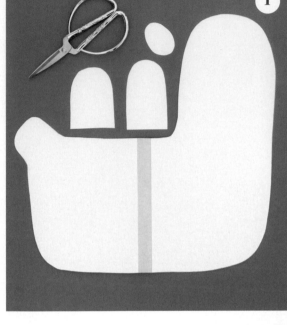

HOW TO MAKE YOUR PLUSH:

1.

Carefully draw and cut out your llama plush templates.

2.

Draw around them on the back of the fun fur fabric.

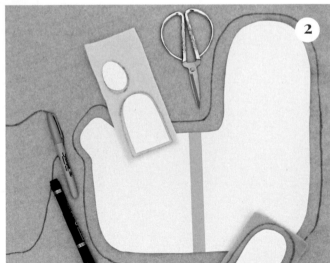

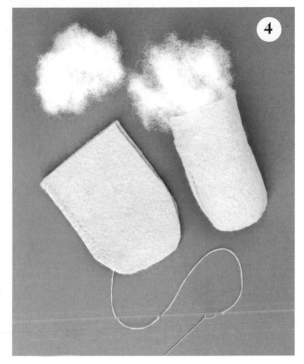

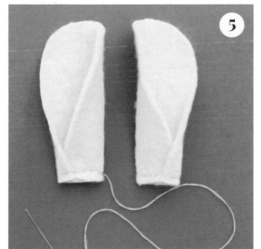

3. Cut out and prepare all the pieces of fabric needed.

4. Stitch around the leg templates as shown, then turn each one inside out and stuff with filling.

5. Fold and stitch the bottom of the llama ears.

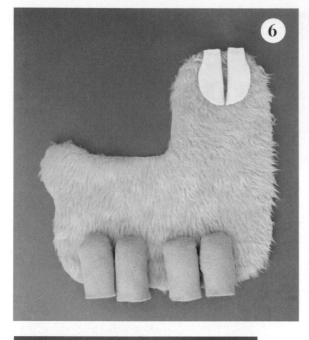

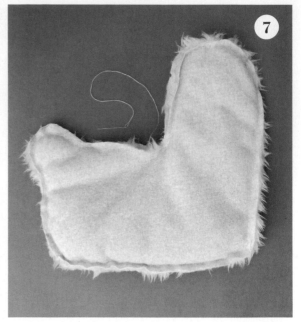

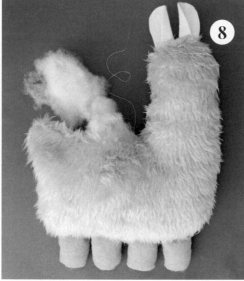

6. Place the finished legs and ears in position on the body of the llama, then carefully fold inward so the edges of the legs and ears will still be on the edge of the body, where they'll be sewn together.

7. Place the second body template over the first and stitch in place, leaving a gap at the top.

8. Turn your llama out the right way. The feet and ears should be in place. Next, stuff the plush as shown and close the gap at the top with a few stitches.

9.

Now to make your llama fringe! Take a length of fun fur fabric and fold it in half. Stitch or glue to secure. Glue the fringe and felt face pieces in place.

10. Collect materials and tassels to decorate your llama plush.

11. Glue or stitch your llama's accessories in place. Adorable!

12. We also made a pom-pom mountain!

YARN-WRAPPED LLAMAS

 ● 60 min.

These lucky yarn-wrapped llamas are inspired by South American worry dolls, traditional dolls made of wire, wool, and colorful textile leftovers.

This is a fun project and best of all, each llama is unique. Experiment with different colors and textures of yarn to create a diverse and colorful family of llamas!

YOU WILL NEED:

Scrap cardboard
Scissors or craft knife
Liquid glue
Masking tape
Colorful wool yarn
Pom-poms and tassels

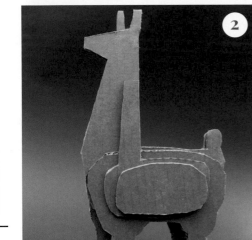

HOW TO MAKE A YARN-WRAPPED LLAMA:

1.

Grab some scrap cardboard, around 2mm thick, and following the templates at the back of the book, cut down the cardboard panels as shown.

2.

Next, glue the panels together using a strong liquid glue or double-sided sticky tape. Make sure your llama can stand up!

3.

Now to start wrapping . . .
Apply a dot of liquid glue to the top of the
ear and attach the length of yarn. Start by
wrapping the yarn tightly around the ears,
tail, and legs.

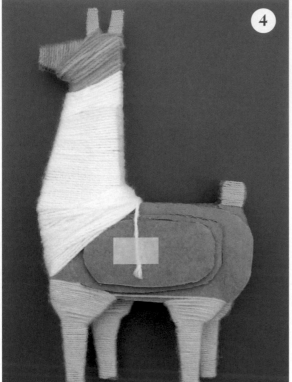

4.

Next, move on to the neck. Stick the end of each colored yarn to the cardboard base with a little masking tape.

5.

Choose another color of yarn and wrap away until you have covered the whole of your llama. Tuck the end of the final length of yarn in to the body of the llama. Apply a little glue to ensure that it stays in place.

PROJECT 6:

LLAMA NECKLACE

 1–2 hours.

Create these adorable necklaces using DIY clay charms, yarn, tassels, and pom-poms. Make your own llama charms using store-bought polymer clay, or by making your own salt dough.

There are lots of easy salt dough recipes—the most basic uses just flour and salt, but you can also add corn starch or white glue to make the dough brighter and less crumbly.

A great activity for a craft party or a fun family afternoon.

YOU WILL NEED:

Polymer clay or DIY salt dough
Yarn in various colors
An embroidery needle
Scissors
Pom-poms and tassels

HOW TO MAKE A LLAMA NECKLACE:

1.

First, mold your clay into the shape of a llama. We also made hearts, cacti, and mountains. If you are using oven-bake clay, follow the instructions on the packet.

If you have made your own salt dough you can bake it or leave it to air-dry overnight. Once your llama is set and cooled you might want to add some paint.

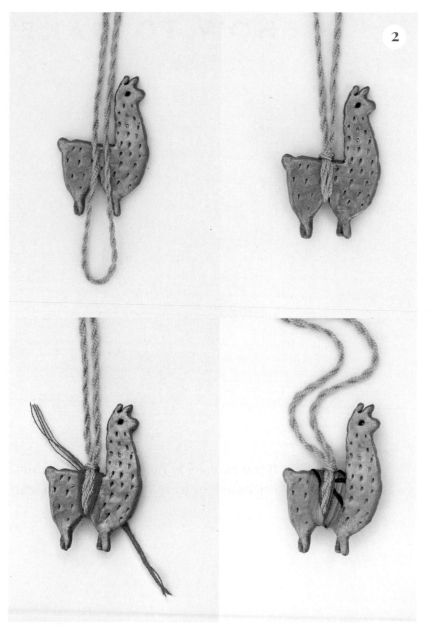

2.

Choose a length of yarn to use as the base of your necklace. You can twirl it to create a plaited effect.

Attach the llama to the yarn by placing a loop over the middle of the llama, then take it around the back to create a slip knot.

Next, wrap colorful threads around and knot at the back to create the saddle.

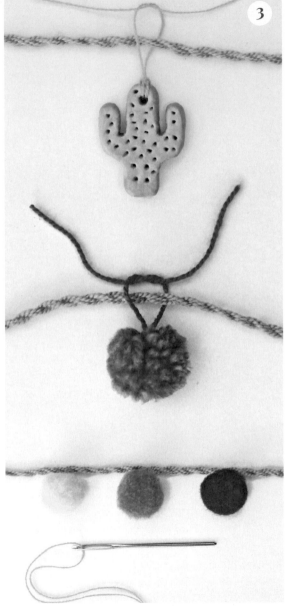

3.

Now to add some more charms, tassels, and pom-poms. You can either tie these on or sew them to the necklace. Add as many as you like to make a vibrant, show-stopping necklace!

4.

Hooray! Your necklace
is ready to wear.
Just tie the ends in a
bow to secure.

LLAMA
DENIM JACKET

  3 hours.

Decorate your own jacket to make a unique fashion statement!
All you will need is a denim jacket, paint, and some imagination
to give an old jacket a new lease on life!

You can use the templates featured in this book,
or create your own design.

YOU WILL NEED:

A denim jacket
Fabric or acrylic paints
Paintbrushes
Masking tape
Permanant marker
Pom-poms

HOW TO MAKE YOUR JACKET:

1.

Prepare your design. As a guide, cut out three panels of paper to the size of your jacket, then sketch out your design on them.

2.

Cut out your images and trace them onto your jacket using a white pencil, or for a lighter jacket you can use a black marker pen.

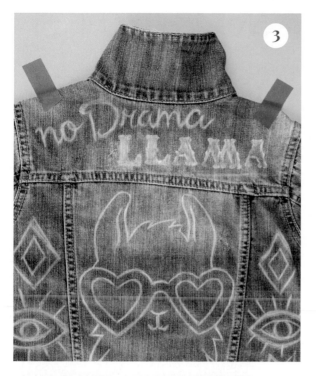

3. Keep going until you have your complete design transferred onto the back of the jacket.

4. Now to start painting! Using small strokes, paint out the base colors of your design. Don't worry if it is not perfect; this will add character!

5. Once the base coat is dry you can outline your images in black to give a more graphic effect.

6. Add a drop shadow to the white text. Use a black permanent marker to add any of the finer detailing and lettering.

7. Lastly, why not add a line of pom-poms or tassels? You can apply these using fabric glue or a few stitches.

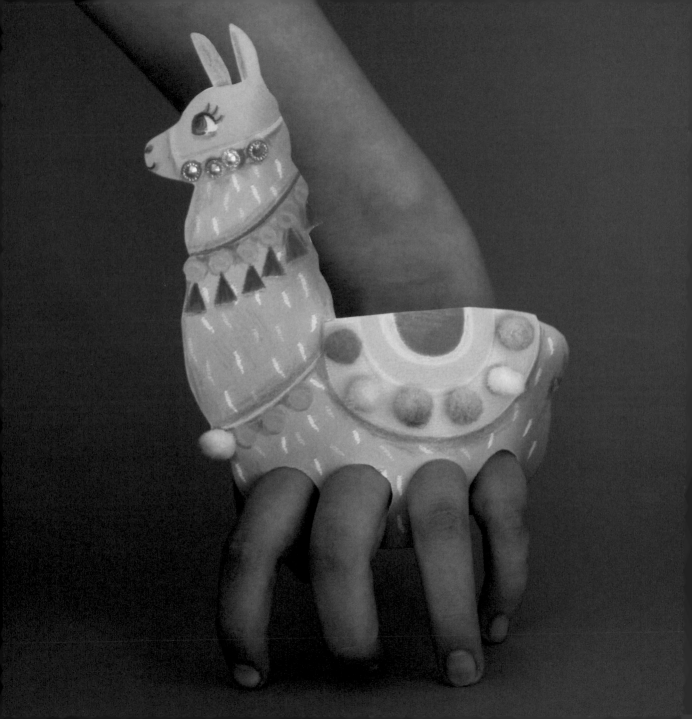

LLAMA
FINGER PUPPETS

  30 min.

Make a family of llama finger puppets!
This project is great for little fingers and can provide hours of fun and creative play.

You can find the templates for this project in the back of the book, or alternatively create your own llama puppet designs!

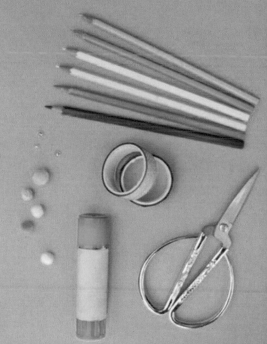

YOU WILL NEED:

Card stock
Scissors
Colored pencils
Sticky gems and pom-poms
Glue stick

1. Color in your llamas. You can use the templates in this book, or create your own llama puppets using the templates as a guide. Be sure to make the puppets the right size to fit your hands!

2. Using your scissors, carefully cut around the llama puppets and finger holes.

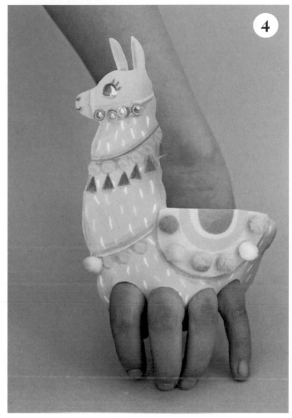

3. Decorate the llamas with sticky gems, pom-poms, or colored tape.

4. Slide your fingers into the leg holes and see your llama come to life!

TIP!

Draw your llama puppets on a
nice thick card stock.
That way they will be sturdier
and last longer!

—

LLAMA
PENNANT BANNERS

 ● 60 min.

Why not fill a wall with these lovely llama-themed pennants?

They are easy and fun to make and really liven up a bedroom
or living room. You can use the templates provided in this book as a base
for your pennants or create your own designs.

Add some fun details with glitter, beads, and tassels
for a really cheery display!

YOU WILL NEED:

Felt in various colors
Glitter foam sheets
Liquid glue
Thread and needles
Scissors
Ribbon and beads
Paper drinking straws

HOW TO MAKE YOUR PENNANTS:

1.

Create your designs, then cut out the base and elements of your llama in felt. For a striking pennant, add an element in glitter.

2.

Start to glue the main elements in place using a strong liquid glue.

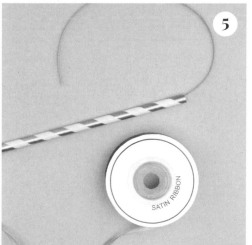

3. Assemble any extra details that you want to add to your pennant. Here we added some little pom-pom parcels for the llama to carry.

4. Add some details to your llama, such as thread, ribbon pom-poms, and beads, to add some texture to your pennant.

5. Next, string a length of ribbon through a colorful drinking straw. Secure the ends with a bow.

6.

Fold the top of your felt pennant base over the drinking straw, then glue or stitch it in place, as shown.

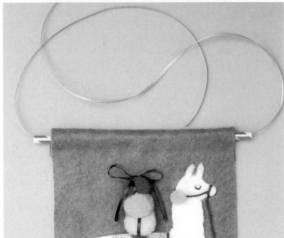

7.

Add any finishing touches, such as a tassel or a a pom-pom ribbon. Yippee! Your pennant is now ready to hang on the wall.

TIP!

Make sure you have a nice sharp pair of scissors to cut your felt. It makes all the difference!

—

NEEDLE-FELTED LLAMAS

🦙🦙🦙🦙🦙 ●● 2 hours.

Our friend Javiera showed us how to make these adorable needle-felted llamas, and trust us, it is a lot easier than you'd imagine.

They are created by sculpting shapes from unspun wool, using special needles to lock the fibers of wool together. Once you get the hang of the technique you can create wonderful characters in no time at all.

This project is not suitable for younger crafters to tackle alone as the needles are very sharp, so please take care!

YOU WILL NEED:

Unspun wool in various colors
Felting needles
A cushion, foam pad, or needle-felting mat
Material for accessories

HOW TO MAKE YOUR LLAMAS:

1.

Calculate how much felt wool you'll need to make your llama. This photo gives you an idea of the length of raw wool you will need to make each ball.

2.

To create the two main balls needed for the body of the llama, roll a strip of wool felt as shown. To achieve a smooth ball, poke or stab the fibers repeatedly with the felting needle, and finally roll it in your hands. The more you poke, the firmer and cleaner-looking your ball will be.

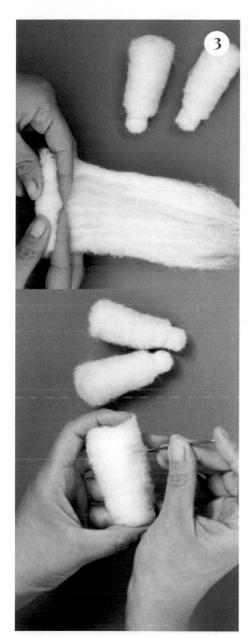

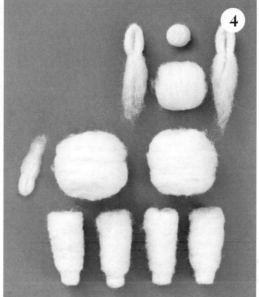

3. To create the legs, roll up a cone of felt wool and secure and shape it with the needle.

4. Create two balls for the body, one for the head, one for the nose, plus four conical legs, two ears (folded wool), and a tail.

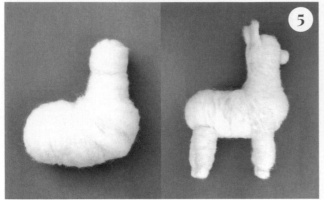

5. To unite the two balls together, take another length of wool and wrap it around the center. Punch the wool with your pin to join them together as shown. Repeat this process with the legs, neck, head, ears, and nose.

6. Now to fill out the body of the llama. Take whisps of raw wool and pin them over the body of the llama to sculpt and pad the shape as shown.

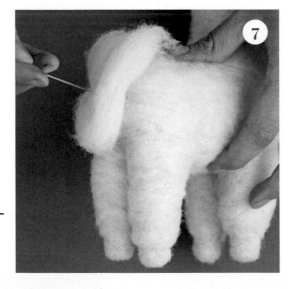

7. Next add the tail, poking it in place with the needle.

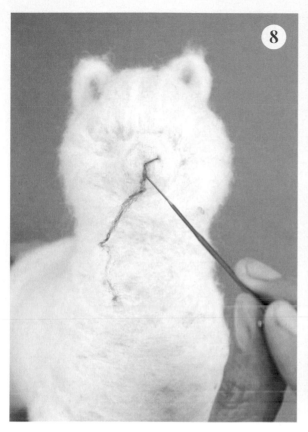

8. Take some small strands of darker wool and carefully pin them in place to create the mouth of the llama.

9. Add the eyes using the same technique. You can also add a little point of white to give the eyes some sparkle.

TIP!

Add some color to your
llama's ears and a cute felt
accessory, like a bow tie
or top hat!

—

LLAMA PINBOARD

3 hours.

I remember having a parrot-shaped pinboard in my bedroom as a child that I was really fond of, and that memory inspired the idea of a llama-shaped pinboard. A pinboard or bulletin board is a perfect and easy way to display photos, invites, notes, and numbers, or keepsakes and momentos.

You can make your own DIY llama-shaped bulletin board or pinboard using cardboard, fabric, and ribbon. This is a no-sew project and you probably have most of the materials on hand in your home!

YOU WILL NEED:

2 large sheets of cardboard
A marker pen
A craft knife
Scissors
Fabric
Fabric Glue
Pom-poms and tassels
Ribbon
Pushpins or tacks
Heavy duty tape

HOW TO MAKE YOUR PINBOARD:

1.

Draw out your llama design out on a sheet of paper the same size as your cardboard. Cut around it and then use it as a template to draw around.

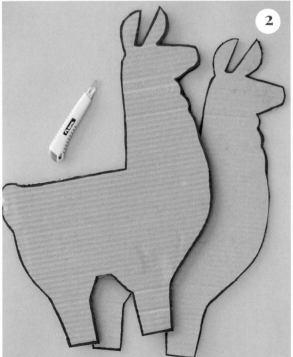

2.

Cut out two identical llamas from your cardboard sheets.

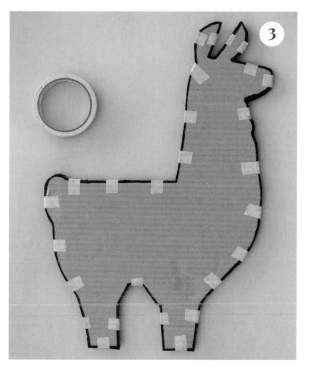

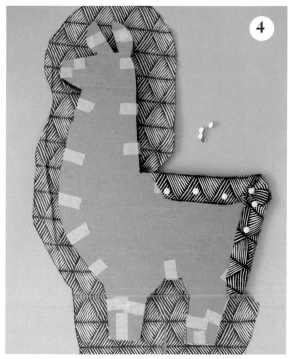

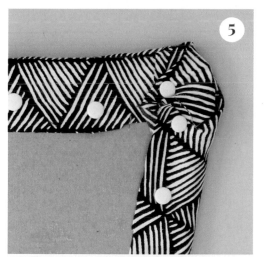

3. Tape the boards securely together.

4. Pick out a fabric and lay the cardboard llama face down on the reverse. Cut **loosely** around the llama shape. Carefully begin to pin the fabric to the back of the llama panel, pulling **tightly** as you pin it in place.

5. Make **small cuts** in the fabric so that it is easier to fold and pin.

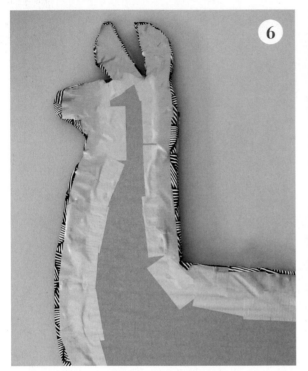

6. Once you have pinned all the way around the llama, secure the fabric to the cardboard using gaffer tape or similar.

7. Choose a contrasting fabric and trim to create the llama's saddle. Cut out a half circle and carefully glue it in place.

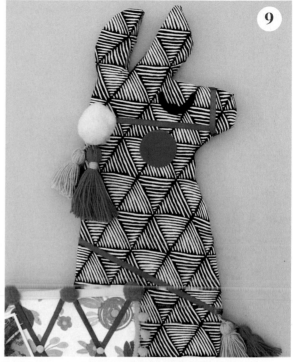

8. Next, carefully lay lengths of colorful ribbon in a criss-cross pattern and attach them to the board using just thumbtacks, so that there is space under each ribbon to slip cards or photos. Trim the ribbons, then cover the edges using ribbon in a contrasting color or texture.

9. Cut out a fabric eye and cheek and glue them in place. Lastly, decorate the head and neck of your llama pinboard with more pom-poms, ribbons, and tassels!

MINI LLAMA BASKETS

  30 min.

These baskets are perfect for party favors, special gifts, or for storing yarn, embroidery thread, and ribbons.

They look super sweet sitting on a shelf or dressing table. Cut out the colorful templates at the back of this book, or copy the black and white templates to create and color your own designs!

You can also add a greeting card or label and an adorable little paper tassel, all included with the templates.

YOU WILL NEED:

Basket templates or colored pens and card stock
Scissors
Glue stick

HOW TO MAKE A LLAMA BASKET:

1.

Cut out your basket templates, or trace or draw your own.

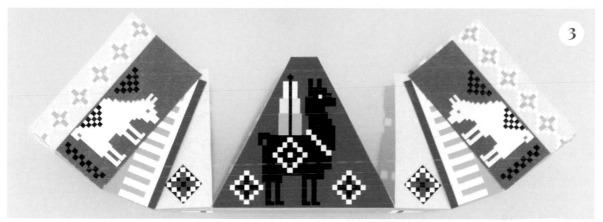

2.

Fold in the panels along each side towards the center.

3.

On either side of the central triangular panel, glue the tips of the three panels together as shown.

4.

Next, attach each group of three side panels to the reverse of the central panel.

5.

Repeat this process on each side to create the basket shape.

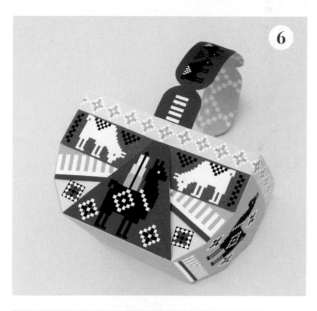

6. Take the handle and glue the ends in place on either side of the inside of the basket.

7. Make a tassel charm. Cut out your tassel template and fringe the end of the bottom rectangle, as shown. Apply a little glue to the top panel and roll it up to make a tassel.

8. Wrap the tassel around the handle of your basket and secure with glue.

LLAMA TASSEL BAG

2 Hours.

Recycle a T-shirt and make this adorable no-sew bag.
This is an easy and fun project. Customize your bag your way,
with tassels, pom-poms, or beads.

Add a DIY llama charm
and step out in style!

YOU WILL NEED:

T-SHIRT BAG
T-Shirt
Scissors
Ruler

BAG CHARM
Felt
Glue
Pom-poms and tassels

HOW TO MAKE
A T-SHIRT BAG:

1.

Take a colorful T-shirt (the larger the better) and lay it flat. Cut off the neck (about 2–3 inches below the neck hemline), sleeves, and bottom hem.

2.

From the base of the shirt, measure up around 6 inches and mark with a length of masking tape. This is where the bottom of your bag will be and where your fringing will start.

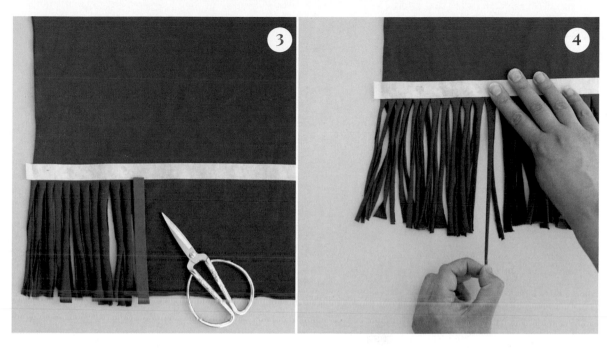

3.

Working from left to right, use scissors to cut strips from the base of the shirt to the tape line. To make the fringing equal, we cut a strip of card stock to use as a guide.

4.

Pull on the bottom of each strip to stretch it to the right length.

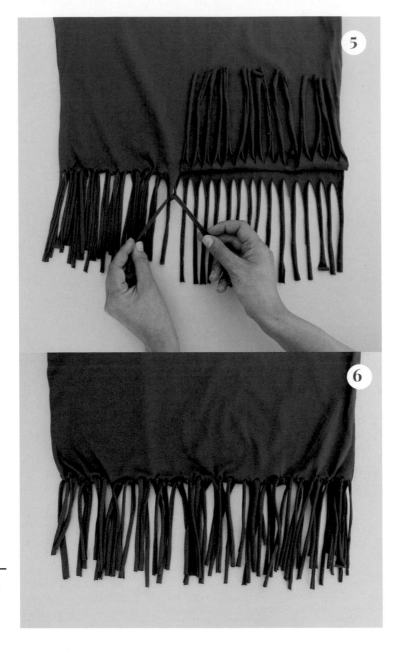

5.

Next, double knot the corresponding front and back pieces of fabric together.

6.

Knot each strand once more with the neighboring strand (so that the strands are knotted in pairs and then with the neighboring pair) to seal the bottom of the bag.

7.

Cut the top of each shoulder strap and tie them together front and back to form the handle of the bag

HOW TO MAKE A TASSEL BAG CHARM:

1.

Create a paper template and cut out two llamas in contrasting colors. You can also cut out a cactus from a glitter foam sheet.

2.

Lay the llamas and cacti back to back, with a length of yarn through the middle of one side. Add cuttings of felt to give your llama charm some body. Glue the charm together using liquid glue or double-sided sticky tape.

3.

Add the felt details using glue. Lastly, attach a loop-topped tassel at the top (see the tutorial in the Techniques section).

HOW TO MAKE A POM-POM BAG CHARM:

1.

Plait together six strands of yarn, parting ¾ of the way down to form two smaller cords.

2.

Create a cardboard-based pom-pom using the technique shown in the back of this book. Slide the cardboard base onto the wool plait as shown.

3.

Cut the sides of the pom-pom
and slide out the cardboard base.

4.

Repeat until your length of
plaited yarn is full of pom-poms!

5.

Now to add your llama charm! Create a loop on the back of the charm (either glue or sew it in place) and slide the plaited yarn through as shown.

LLAMA PIN BROOCHES

  60 min.

These loopy llama pins are super easy to make. You can use the color templates in this book, or color in the black and white versions your way. Add pom-poms, gems, or glitter.

Make as many as you can and cover a jacket, pencil case, or bag with these fun, happy pins! Give them to your friends as gifts or party favors.

YOU WILL NEED:

Pin brooch templates
Colored pens and pencils
Contact paper
Sticky tape
Safety pins
Pom-poms and glitter

HOW TO MAKE YOUR PINS:

1.

Cut out your llama pin templates in this book, or draw your own versions.
If you chose the black and white templates, color them in using bright colors.

2.

Carefully lay the templates on a sheet of contact paper.

3.

Lay another sheet of contact paper on top, so that the images are sealed.

4.

Carefully cut around each llama image. Next, decorate the plus with pom-poms and glitter tape.

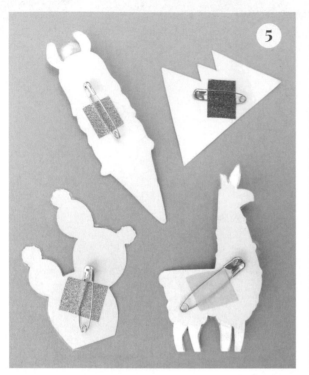

5. Flip the templates over and, using a little tape, attach a safety pin to the reverse of each one to create your pin brooches.

6. Hooray, your pins are ready! Perfect to decorate a denim jacket, or school bag, or to give as gifts to your friends.

LLAMA PIÑATA

  2 Hours.

Make your own adorable piñata for a fiesta or as a cute decoration for your home. Fill it with candies, treats, and confetti, then pull the tassel to release the fun!

Piñatas are fun to make—use old boxes to construct your llama, then cover it with fringed tissue paper.

YOU WILL NEED:

Cardboard boxes
Tissue paper
Scissors
Glue stick
Sticky tape
Yarn
Candy!

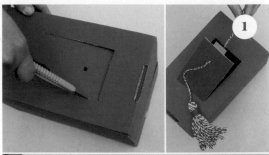

HOW TO MAKE
A LLAMA PIÑATA:

1.

Choose a box as the body of your llama piñata. Cut a "trap door" on one side. Add a small tab to keep it shut, then thread a length of yarn through the center of the door and secure with a small stick (or tape), as shown.

2.

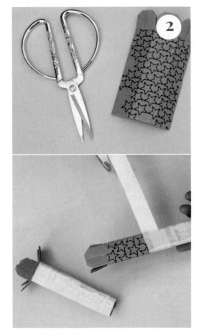

Next, make your llama legs. Cut out four identical rectangles out of scrap cardboard. Fold each one into three panels and cut tabs at one end. Wrap with tape to secure.

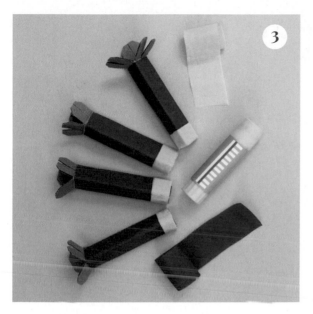

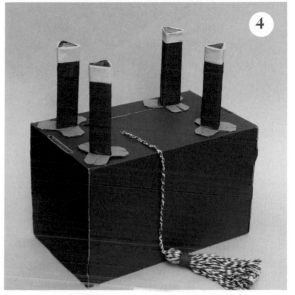

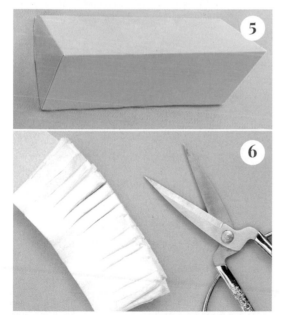

3. Wrap colored tissue paper or tape around each leg.

4. Attach the legs to the body of the llama using glue or double-sided sticky tape.

5. Cut the corner edge off a second box to use as the llama's neck.

6. Trim long strips of white tissue paper into fringing as shown.

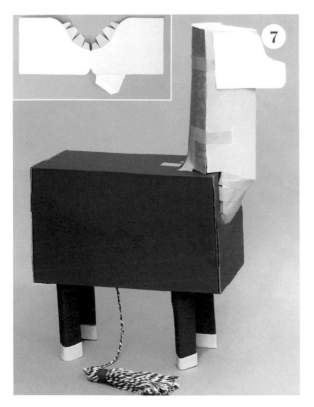

7. Using the template at the back of the book, cut the face of the llama out of white card stock. Attach the neck and face to the llama body using tape as shown, so that the front of the neck juts out from the body. Use another piece of scrap cardboard to form the back of the llama's neck.

8. Starting at the bottom of the llama's body, wrap the fringed tissue paper around the box, sticking it in place with a glue stick. Layer the strips of tissue paper close together.

9. When you reach the top of the box, lay the fringing flat on each side and work inwards, meeting in the middle.

10. Continue to wrap the fringe around the neck of the llama. Work around the edge of the face and add a plume of fringing on the top of the head.

11.

Cut two ears from white card stock and glue them to each side of the llama head. Then, using colored tape or paper, add an eye and a rosy cheek. Finish off with some decorations. We added ribbon, tassels, and a fabric saddle. You can fill your llama with goodies or use it is a party centerpiece! If you would like to hang your llama piñata up, tie a colorful ribbon around its middle, making a loop at the top.

12.

Open the trap door to fill your piñata with candies and goodies, then close it carefully. Just pull the tassel to release!

13.

Use the cactus template at the back of the book to make these adorable mini cactus piñatas too. Starting at the bottom, wrap your cactus with green tissue paper, with the fringing pointing up, to create spikes!

LLAMA CRAFTS

LLAMA GARLANDS

 1.5 Hours

Decorate your home or a party with this adorable llama garland.
Paint your own llamas and add tassels and cacti for a vibrant decoration.

Store your garland carefully and use it year after year!

YOU WILL NEED:

Colorful paints
Sticky tape
White card stock
Scissors
Ribbon
Yarn

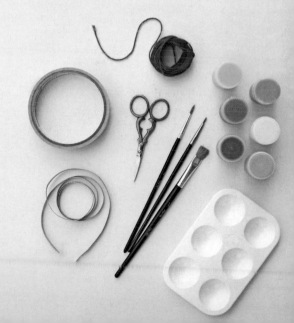

HOW TO MAKE
YOUR GARLANDS:

1.

Copy or cut out the garland templates in the back of the book, or create your own!

2.

Paint the llamas and cactus templates with vibrant colors.

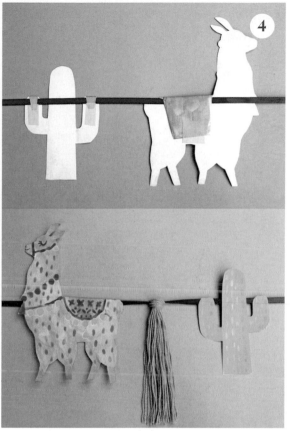

3. Collect and arrange all the templates and fold over the tabs at the top.

4. Fold the tabs over a length of ribbon and secure in place with a little sticky tape. Add a colorful yarn tassel between each template.

HOORAY!

Your garland is ready
to hang on the wall.

—

LLAMA MASKS

 1 Hour.

Make a lovely llama mask using the vibrant templates in this book, or color in and create your own version!

The masks are easy and fun to make and perfect for a costume party or imaginative play time. Have fun!

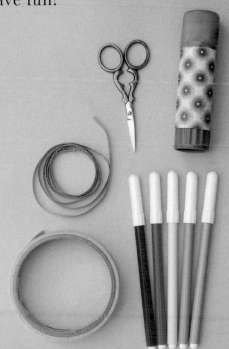

YOU WILL NEED:

Mask template
Scissors
Glue stick
Masking tape
Ribbon

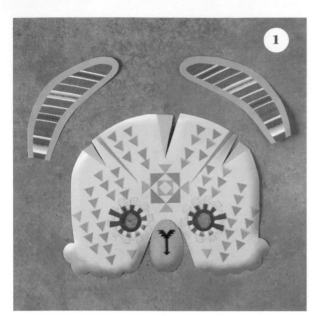

HOW TO MAKE YOUR MASKS:

1.

Carefully cut out the llama mask template.

2.

Glue the middle panels together with your glue stick. Next, stick the two side panels together.

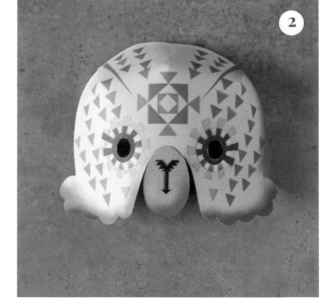

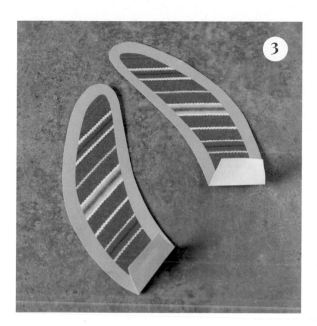

3. Fold the tabs on the llama ears, ready to stick onto the mask.

4. Add the ears to your llama mask.

5. Attach a length of ribbon to either side of your mask. Stick it in place with masking tape.

6. Tie the ribbon in a bow at the back of your head.

HOORAY!

You're a llama!

COOKIE RECIPE:

2 cups plain flour
½ cup butter
½ cup sugar
2 spoonfuls of honey
1 spoonful of cocoa powder
½ teaspoon vanilla extract

Mix together and bake on a
medium heat for 10 minutes
or until golden brown.

LLAMA ICE CREAM SANDWICHES

2 hours.

Why not make these delicious llama-shaped ice cream sandwiches for your next fiesta! Decorate them with sweet patterns and colorful sprinkles.

Our friend Jo created a delicious cookie recipe for you. The honey makes them chewy and delicious and just the right texture to hold the ice cream. Yummy!

YOU WILL NEED:

Ice cream
Cookie ingredients (see recipe)
Sprinkles
Cookie cutters

HOW TO MAKE YOUR COOKIES:

1.

The first step is to prepare your cookie dough and roll it out to approximately 4mm in height.

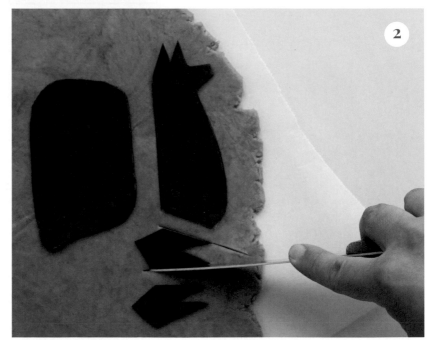

2.

Cut out the llama stencils on durable card stock, place them on the cookie dough, and cut around them using a sharp knife. Remember to cut out two body shapes for each llama.

LLAMA CRAFTS

3. Once you have cut out your cookie stencils you can decorate them. We used cookie cutters and kebab sticks to gently press into the dough. Next, bake your cookies for 20 minutes in the oven.

4. Let the llama cookies cool completely.

5. Carefully spoon ice cream onto one side of your llama cookie. Make sure the ice cream is straight from the freezer so it is not too runny.

6. Place the other cookie on top to create a sandwich and smooth the ice cream with the back of a spoon.

7. Next dip the edges of the sandwich in sprinkles so that they stick to the ice cream.

8. Now to add the llama's head and legs. Gently press them into the ice cream as shown. Once they are all ready, place your llama ice cream sandwiches in the freezer for 1 hour.

9.

Your llama ice cream
sandwiches are ready
to serve!

TECHNIQUES

You might have noticed that this book contains a whole lot of pom-poms and tassels!
On the following pages we will show you various techniques for making your own.
They are surprisingly easy and fun to make.

POM-POMS

1. Wrap the yarn around your hands approximately one hundred times to make a nice, fluffy pom-pom.

2. Carefully slide the coil of yarn off your hand.

3. Tie a length of yarn around the center of the coil, as tightly as you can, securing with a double knot.

4. Wrap the length around several times before securing with a double knot and trimming the ends.

5. Cut through the bottom of the wrapped yarn to create your pom-pom.

6. Lastly, neatly trim your pom-pom to your preferred length. Hooray, your pom-pom is ready!

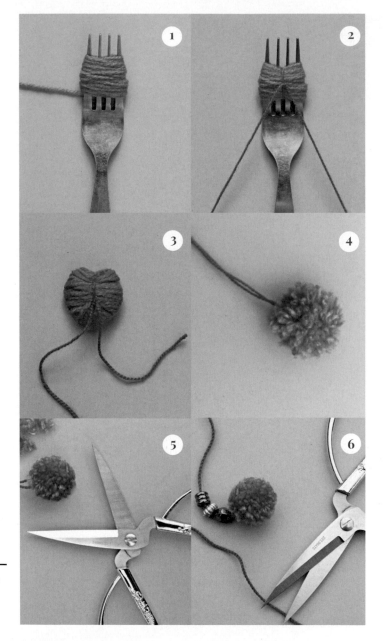

MINI POM-POMS

1. Wrap the yarn around the fork as shown approximately fifty times to make a nice, fluffy pom-pom.

2. Tie a length of yarn or thread around the center of the coil of wool, as tightly as you can, securing with a double knot. It makes things easier, and also looks nice, if this thread is of a different color.

3. Carefully slide the coil of yarn off the fork.

4. Now take your scissors and cut through the two loops of yarn on either side.

5. Your mini pom-pom will be wild and wooly! Time for a haircut. Be careful not to trim through the thread.

6. Trim carefully around the pom-pom until you have an even, round ball. Roll it in your hands to finish off.

CARDBOARD POM-POMS

1. Use scraps of cardboard to create two identical C-shaped rings, as shown.

2. Wrap your yarn around the cardboard rings. Keep going until it is nice and plump.

3. Start snipping through the wrapped yarn, all along the edge of the rings.

4. Next, cut a length of yarn and tie it around the middle of the pom-pom, in between the two cardboard rings.

5. Wrap it around twice, pulling the yarn as tight as you can, then secure with a double knot.

6. Carefully remove the cardboard template. If you need to, trim your pom-pom to even out the shape.

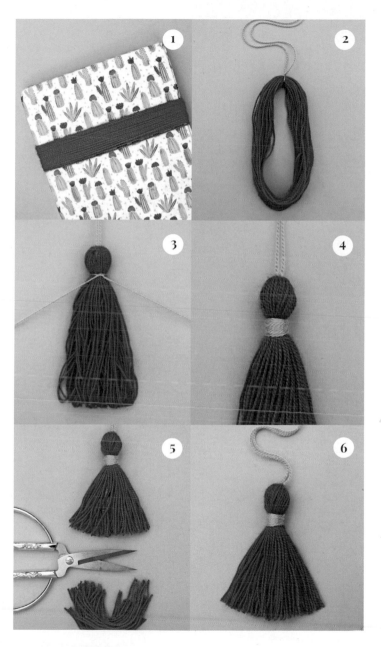

TASSELS

1. Wrap yarn around a small book or a piece of stiff cardboard between twenty and forty times, depending on how full you want your tassel to be.

2. Slip the looped yarn off the book and tie a length of thread around the top, securing with a double knot.

3. Tie another length of yarn around the top of the tassel as shown, approximately 8mm from the top, and secure with a knot.

4. Wrap the length around several times before securing with a double knot and trimming the ends.

5. Cut through the bottom of the wrapped yarn to create your tassel.

6. Lastly, neatly trim your tassel to your preferred length. Hooray, your tassel is ready!

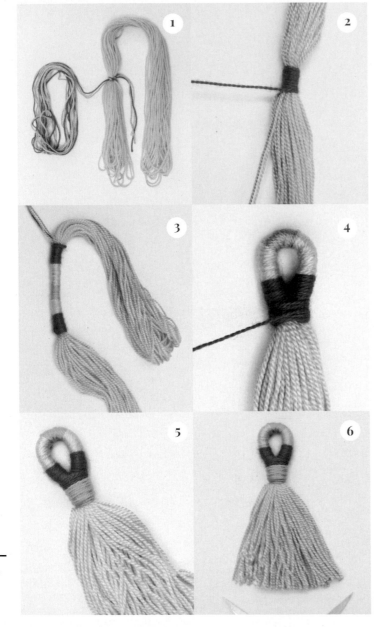

LOOP-TOPPED TASSELS

1. To form the main tassel, choose a yarn and measure out fifty loops of approximately 14 inches.

2. Take 3 lengths of colored yarn (approximately 16 inches) and tie one end of each to the original looped yarn, about a third of the way from the end.

3. After around every half inch, swap colors and keep wrapping until you have an even bunch on either side. Cut off two of the three strands.

4. Bend the center wrapped portion (as shown) and wrap the remaining strand around both sides approximately thirty times. Secure with a knot.

5. For a tidy tassel, wrap another colored thread around the center as shown.

6. Snip off the ends of the looped yarn to create your tassel!

TEMPLATES

In this section you can find templates for some of the projects in this book. The color templates are ready to cut out and use, so that you can get crafting straight away!

The black and white templates are for tracing, scanning, or photocopying. Some should be resized to the right size for your project.

PROJECT 8: LLAMA FINGER PUPPETS

PROJECT 12: LLAMA BASKETS

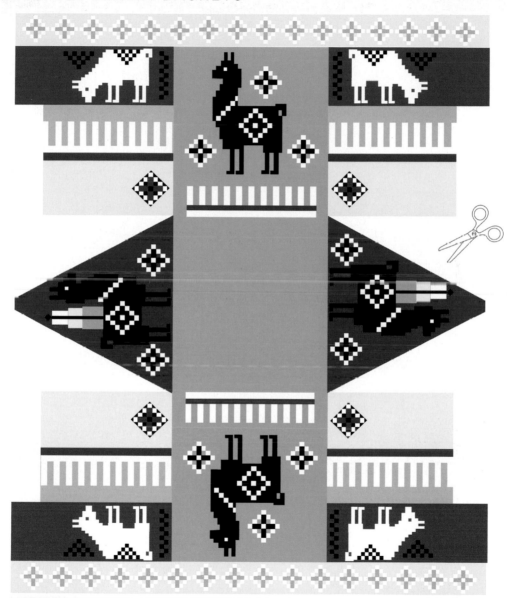

PROJECT 12: LLAMA BASKETS

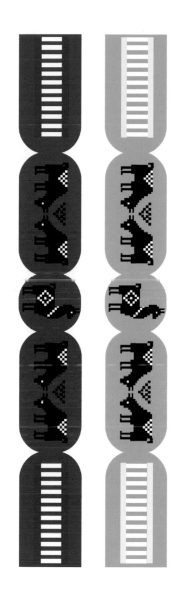

PROJECT 15: MINI CACTUS PIÑATAS

PROJECT 1: HAPPY LLAMA STAMPERS

PROJECT 5: YARN-WRAPPED LLAMAS

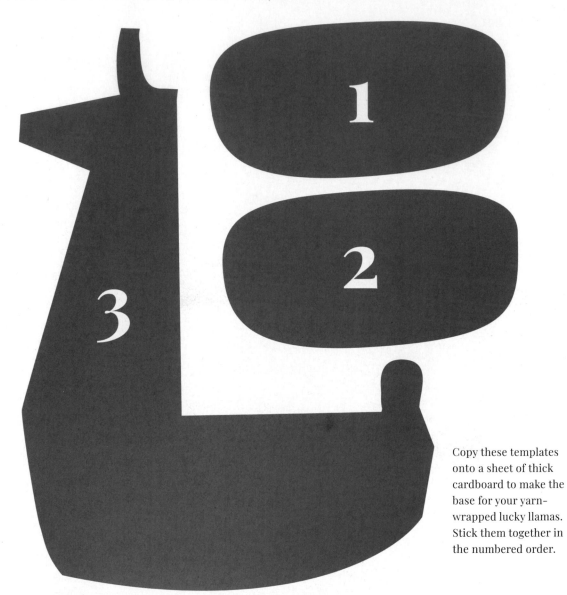

Copy these templates onto a sheet of thick cardboard to make the base for your yarn-wrapped lucky llamas. Stick them together in the numbered order.

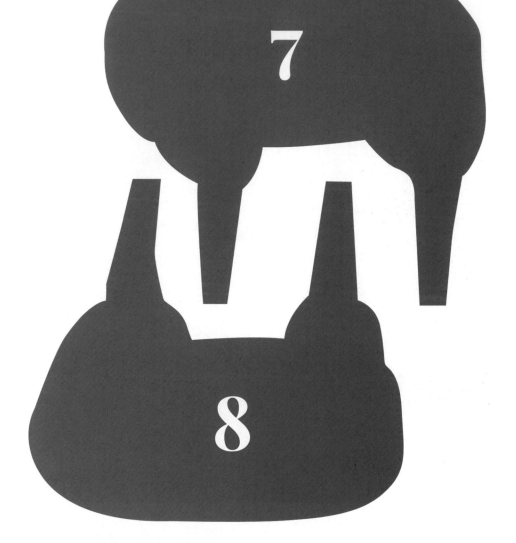

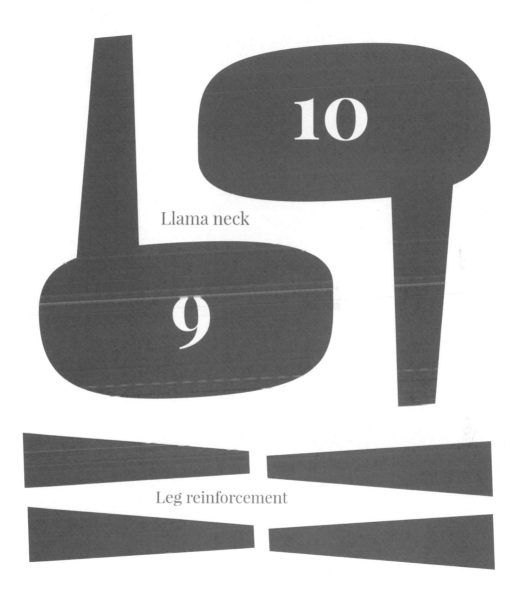

Llama neck

10

9

Leg reinforcement

LLAMASTE

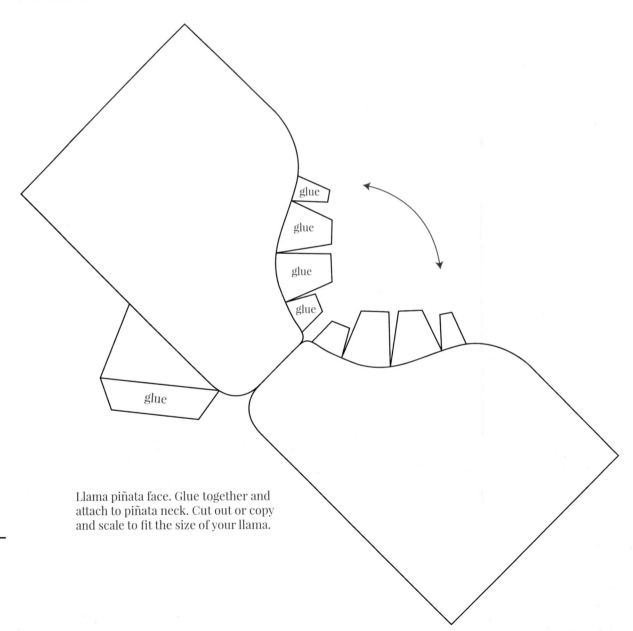

glue

glue

glue

glue

glue

Llama piñata face. Glue together and attach to piñata neck. Cut out or copy and scale to fit the size of your llama.

PROJECT 8: LLAMA FINGER PUPPETS

PROJECT 12: LLAMA BASKETS

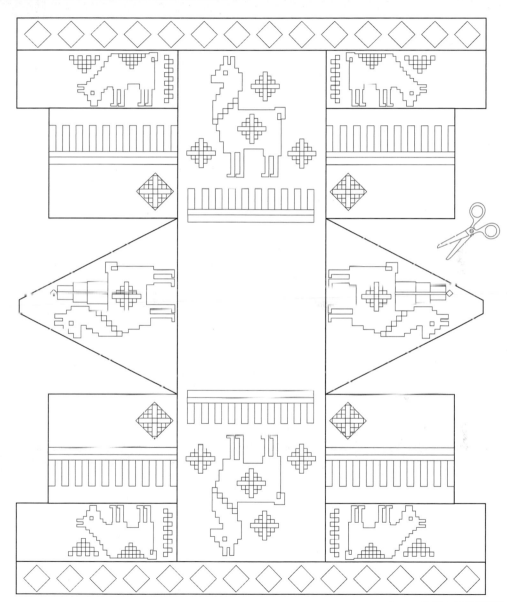

PROJECT 12: LLAMA BASKETS

PROJECT 16: LLAMA GARLANDS

Decorate your llamas, then fold the tabs over a length of ribbon to create a garland.

glue

glue

glue

glue

glue

WITH THANKS TO

Harvey and Missy, our inspiration for Happythought!
Our wonderful models Anouk, Leon, Cael, Ali, Arai, Carolina, Vicente, and Sofi;
Bahdra Meyer for the use of her beautiful house; Tilly for her garden and tea;
Jason Schneider and Jesse McHugh at Racehorse Publishing; Rose Deakin
for her llama research; and to all our family for their love and support.

CREDITS

Creative Direction: Ellen Deakin.
Design and Layout: Antonia Orrego Requena.
Crafts: Ellen Deakin, Javiera Isabel Gallardo Varas,
Antonia Lopez Martinez, Antonia Orrego Requena.
Photography: Pilar Castro Evensen,
Diego Astorga Carneyro, and Ellen Deakin.
Baking: Maria Josefina Gallardo Varas.
Production: Harry Olden.

ABOUT THE AUTHOR

An avid crafter since childhood, Ellen trained in design at the renowned Glasgow School of Art, then went on to work in the UK as a graphic designer, illustrator, and art director.

In 2010, along with her husband Harry Olden, she launched Happythought, a craft website full of inspiring ideas, tutorials, and fun printable projects.

At Happythought, the emphasis is on producing craft templates that, as well as being lovely to look at, are easy to make, with the minimum fuss and maximum fun! Ellen and Harry split their time between the UK and Chile, and have two children, Harvey and Missy.

You can find lots of fun paper craft projects, party printables, craft inspiration, and tutorials at happythought.co.uk